Peter Ilyich Tchaikovsky

Concerto No. 1 for Piano and Orchestra in B♭ minor / b-Moll

Op. 23

Edited by / Herausgegeben von
Richard Clarke

EULENBURG

Contents / Inhalt

EAS 147
ISBN 978-3-7957-6547-7
ISMN M-2002-2371-2

© 2007 Ernst Eulenburg & Co GmbH, Mainz
for Europe excluding the British Isles
Ernst Eulenburg Ltd, London
for all other countries
Edition based on Eulenburg Study Score ETP 709
CD ℗ & © 2004 Naxos Rights International Ltd

Ernst Eulenburg Ltd
48 Great Marlborough Street
London W1F 7BB

Preface

Dedicated to Hans von Bülow
Composed: 1875 in Kamenka
First performance: 25 October 1875, Boston, soloist: Hans von Bülow,
conductor: Benjamin Johnson Lang
First publication: P. I. Jurgenson, Moscow, 1875 (orchestral parts
and version for 2 pianos) and August 1879 (full score)
Orchestration: 2 flutes, 2 oboes, 2 clarinets, 2 bassoons – 4 horns,
2 trumpets, 3 trombones – timpani – solo piano – strings
Duration: ca. 34 minutes

The earliest mention of the B flat minor Piano Concerto occurs in a letter from Tchaikovsky to his brother Modest on 29 October/10 November 1874: 'I should like to start work on a piano concerto'. Eleven years later he wrote to the publisher Bessel: 'I'm beginning to shape a big new work which has dominated all my thoughts ever since I finished the vocal score of the opera [*Vakula the Smith*]'. Other letters to his brothers during the next month or so give us glimpses of the composer at work:

'I'm now completely immersed in the composition of the piano concerto. I am particularly anxious that [Nikolai] Rubinstein should play it at his concert; the thing moves very slowly and doesn't come at all easily. […] I force my brain to think out piano passages.' (21 November/3 December 1874)

'I'm submerged with all my soul in the composition of the piano concerto; the thing is advancing, but very badly.' (26 November/9 December 1874)

'I work unceasingly on the concerto, which I must finish this week without fail.' (undated, mid-December 1874)

It was actually completed, though with the orchestral part only as yet for a second piano, on 21 December 1874/2 January 1875, and the urgency was owing to the circumstances that Tchaikovsky wished to play it to Nikolai Rubinstein on Christmas Eve. How he did so and how cruelly Rubinstein criticised it, he told at great length to Mme von Meck three years later in a letter (21 January/2 February 1878) which Modest Tchaikovsky first published in his great biography of his brother and which has been quoted many times since. Commenting on the letter, Modest says, 'Peter Ilyich crossed out on the score the dedication of the concerto to

N. Rubinstein and in place of his name put that of Hans von Bülow', and this story has often been repeated. But the 'score' did not yet exist; it was not completed until 9/21 February – the piano part being copied in by another hand – and the crossed-out dedication on it was not to Rubinstein but 'to Sergei Ivanovich Taneiev'.

The change of dedication was a matter not of pique but of expediency. Taneiev was 18 and still a student at the Moscow Conservatoire; Bülow was a world-famous pianist. And he was genuinely flattered by the dedication. He thanked Tchaikovsky in a long and gushing letter in French (1 June 1875) in which he speaks of the concerto as 'so original in thought (yet never affected), so noble, so strong, so interesting in details (the quantity of which never interferes with the clearness and unity of the conception as a whole). [...] In short, this is a real pearl and you deserve the gratitude of all pianists'. More importantly, he immediately took the concerto to America and gave the first performance of it in the Boston Music Hall on 25 October 1875, when the conductor was Benjamin Johnson Lang. The first performance in Russia was given in St Petersburg 19 days later by Gustav Kross, with Napravnik conducting. This was ruined by too fast tempos, but the first Moscow performance, on 21 November/3 December, was a model one with Taneiev as soloist, and as conductor – Nikolai Rubinstein. (In 1878 Rubinstein began to perform it as soloist.) England heard the concerto soon afterwards (23 March 1876), when Eduard Dannreuther played it at the Crystal Palace, London, and Germany on 17 June 1876 (played at Wiesbaden by von Bülow).

Smarting under Rubinstein's original criticisms, Tchaikovsky had declared, 'I won't alter a single note; I shall print it exactly as it is now'. And Jurgenson did publish the orchestral parts and the version for 2 pianos in 1875 in the original form. But directly after the first Moscow performance Tchaikovsky began to contemplate alterations and wrote to von Bülow to tell him so. Von Bülow replied:

'You write to me that you want to make some changes in your concerto? I shall, of course, receive them with great interest – but I should like to express my opinion that they are not at all necessary – except some enrichment of the piano part in certain *tuttis*, which I took it upon myself to make, as I did in Raff's concerto also. And allow me one other observation: the great effect of the finale loses something if the triumph of the second motif before the last *stretta* is played 'molto meno mosso'.'

Dannreuther was bolder. He not only 'made changes in the piano part to heighten its effectiveness, without interfering with the composer's intentions', but had the temerity to tell Tchaikovsky what he had done. However, the composer took this in good part, thanked Dannreuther for his 'very sensible and practical suggestions', and assured him that he would adopt them 'if there is any question of a second edition of my concerto' (letter of 18/30 March 1876). Actually the original version was never published in score until it appeared as Volume 28 of the Tchaikovsky Complete Edition in 1955; Jurgenson did not bring out a full score until August 1879, when it was described as a second edition 'revised and corrected by the composer'. A genuine 'second edition' of the 2-piano version was issued at the same time in conformity with this. The changes concern only the layout of the piano part in the first movement and may well embody Dannreuther's suggestions, the originals of which are lost.

During the period December 1888 – February 1889, Tchaikovsky prepared a third edition of the concerto, in consultation with Ziloti who had become one of its best exponents. In this, besides minor alterations in the introduction to the first movement and in the finale, he made a major change in the finale: the substitution of five bars (109–113 in the present edition, which follows the definitive version) for a passage of 17 bars – which Tchaikovsky had jestingly called 'die verfluchte Stelle' – in which the skipping figure of the piano appeared all over the orchestra (letter to Ziloti, 27 December 1888/8 January 1889). The same letter shows that, for the performance he had conducted at Hamburg nearly a year before with Sapelnikov, Tchaikovsky temporarily took out this 'skipping figure' altogether. The third edition of the concerto was published at the end of 1889 or the beginning of 1890.

Many of the changes made by Tchaikovsky concern tempo-markings: for instance, the original marking of the famous introduction was *Andante non troppo*. The time-signature of the ensuing *Allegro* was corrected in pencil by the composer from **C** to **¢**; but his intention is not clear, for his bilingual instruction to the conductor to 'beat 2 in a bar' (because of the crotchet triplets) occurs much later, at the point where the marking *Alla breve* and the new time-signature now appear. A number of the present tempo-modifications are translations of Tchaikovsky's blue-pencil additons to the autograph MS: e.g. *plus lent* at bar 186 of the first movement, which now appears as *Poco meno mosso*. The marking *Sostenuto molto* at bar 101 of the Finale – the first appearance of the 'skipping figure' – appears in neither autograph nor first edition. Nor does *Tempo I ma tranquillo* at bar 214; but an unknown hand has written *Tempo I* in the autograph and Tchaikovsky added *mais peu plus lent*. However, not all Tchaikovsky's pencillings were given the permanence of print; among these may be mentioned the repeated injunction not to hurry (*ne pressez pas le mouvement*) at bars 420 and 425 of the first movement. In the original edition the middle section of the second movement is marked not *Prestissimo* but *Allegro vivace assai*, and there is extant a letter from Taneiev to K. N. Igumnov in 1912 (printed in *Sovetskaya Muzika*, 1946, No. 1, pp. 88–9) in which he protests that this is the correct tempo, that *Prestissimo* is too fast.

It is generally known, from Modest's biography, that this section is based on a French *chansonette*, 'Il faut s'amuser, danser et rire', 'which my brother Anatol and I were constantly singing at the beginning of the 70s', and that the first *Allegro* theme of the concerto is part of a tune sung by blind, so-called 'lyre singers' in the Ukraine:

The first theme of the finale is also derived from a Ukranian folk-song which Tchaikovsky found in Rubets's 'Sbornik ukrainskikh narodnikh pesen' (St Petersburg 1872):

Viy-di, viy - di ___ I - van - ku! ___ Zas-pi-vay nam ___

Gerald Abraham

Vorwort

Komponiert: 1874 in Kamenka
Uraufführung: 25. Oktober 1875 in Boston, Solist: Hans von Bülow,
Dirigent: Benjamin Johnson Lang
Originalverlag: P. I. Jurgenson, Moskau, 1875 (Orchesterstimmen
und Bearbeitung für 2 Klaviere), und August 1879 (Partitur)
Orchesterbesetzung: 2 Flöten, 2 Oboen, 2 Klarinetten, 2 Fagotte –
4 Hörner, 2 Trompeten, 3 Posaunen – Pauken – Soloklavier – Streicher
Spieldauer: etwa 34 Minuten

Die erste Erwähnung des Klavier-Konzerts in b-Moll findet sich in einem Brief Tschaikows-kys an seinen Bruder Modest vom 29. Oktober/10. November 1874: „Ich möchte gern ein Klavier-Konzert in Angriff nehmen." Elf Tage später schrieb er an den Verleger Bessel: „Ich fange an, ein neues, großes Werk zu gestalten, das meine Gedanken beherrscht, seitdem ich den Klavier-Auszug der Oper [*Wakula der Schmied*] beendet habe." Andere Briefe des Komponisten an seine Brüder aus den nächsten Monaten zeigen den Komponisten bei der Arbeit:

„Ich bin jetzt ganz in die Komposition des Klavier-Konzertes versunken. Vor allem wünsche ich mir, dass [Nikolai] Rubinstein es in seinem Konzert spielt; die Sache geht langsam vor-wärts und ist nicht leicht. […] Ich strenge mein Gehirn an, Klavier-Passagen auszudenken." (21. November/3. Dezember)

„Ich bin mit ganzer Seele in die Komposition des Klavier-Konzertes vertieft; die Sache geht vorwärts, aber nicht gut." (26. November/8. Dezember)

„Ich arbeite unablässig an dem Klavier-Konzert, das ich bestimmt diese Woche fertig stellen muss." (Mitte Dezember)

Tatsächlich war es beendet am 21. Dezember/2. Januar, wenn auch das Orchester zunächst auf einem 2. Klavier skizziert war, weil Tschaikowsky es am Weihnachtsabend Nikolai Rubin-stein vorspielen wollte. Wie er das tat und wie hart Rubinstein es kritisierte, hat er drei Jahre später in einem Brief an Frau von Meck (21. Januar/2. Februar 1878) berichtet, den Modest Tschaikowsky erstmals in seiner großen Biographie seines Bruders veröffentlichte und der seitdem oft zitiert wurde. Hierzu sagt Modest: „Peter Iljitsch hat auf der Partitur die Wid-mung an Rubinstein gestrichen und an die Stelle den Namen von Hans von Bülow gesetzt." Diese Geschichte ist oft wiedererzählt worden. Aber die „Partitur" existierte noch gar nicht.

Sie wurde erst am 9./21. Februar beendet – mit Eintragung der Klavierstimme von anderer Hand – und die gestrichene Widmung galt nicht Rubinstein, sondern lautete „an Sergej Iwanowitsch Tanejew".

Die Änderung der Widmung erfolgte nicht aus Zorn, sondern aus Zweckmäßigkeit. Tanejew war erst 18 Jahre alt und studierte noch am Konservatorium in Moskau, während Bülow bereits ein weltberühmter Pianist war. Dieser war aufrichtig geschmeichelt von der Widmung und dankte Tschaikowsky in einem langen und überschwänglichen Brief in französischer Sprache (1. Juni 1875). Er spricht darin von dem Konzert als „so originell in den Gedanken (aber niemals gekünstelt), so vornehm, so stark, so interessant in den Details (deren Menge niemals die Klarheit und die Einheit des Entwurfs im Ganzen stört). [...] Kurz, es ist eine wirkliche Perle, und Sie verdienen den Dank aller Pianisten." Wichtiger als diese Worte ist, dass er das Werk sofort nach Amerika mitnahm und es am 25. Oktober in der Music Hall Boston unter Leitung von Benjamin Johnson Lang aufführte. Die erste Aufführung in Russland fand 19 Tage später durch Gustav Kross unter Napravnik in St. Petersburg statt. Diese Aufführung litt unter zu raschen Tempi, aber die erste Aufführung in Moskau am 21. November/3. Dezember mit Tanejew als Solisten und N. Rubinstein als Dirigenten war musterhaft. (1878 begann Rubinstein auch selbst, das Konzert zu spielen.) England hörte das Werk bald darauf (23. März 1876) mit Edward Dannreuther im Londoner Crystal Palace und Deutschland am 17. Juni 1876, gespielt von Bülow in Wiesbaden.

Gekränkt durch Rubinsteins ursprüngliche Kritik hatte Tschaikowsky erklärt: „Ich will nicht eine Note ändern; ich will es drucken genau so, wie es ist." Und Jurgenson gab die Stimmen und die Bearbeitung für zwei Klaviere 1875 genau in dieser Form heraus. Aber gleich nach der ersten Moskauer Aufführung begann er über Änderungen nachzudenken und schrieb darüber an Bülow. Dieser antwortete:

„Sie schreiben, Sie wollen Änderungen in Ihrem Konzert vornehmen? Ich werde diese natürlich mit großem Interesse studieren, aber ich möchte doch sagen, dass ich solche durchaus nicht für nötig halte – ausgenommen eine gewisse Bereicherung der Solostimme in einigen *tutti*, die ich mir selbst erlaubt habe zu machen, wie ich es auch bei dem Konzert von Raff getan habe. Und erlauben Sie mir eine andere Bemerkung: die große Wirkung des Finale verliert etwas, wenn der Triumph des 2. Themas, vor der letzten *Stretta* ‚Molto meno mosso' gespielt wird."

Dannreuther war kühner. Er „machte nicht nur Änderungen in der Solostimme um die Wirkung zu erhöhen, ohne gegen die Absichten des Komponisten zu verstoßen", sondern war dreist genug, ihm das mitzuteilen. Tschaikowsky indessen nahm das gutmütig hin und dankte Dannreuther für seine „verständigen und praktischen Vorschläge". Er wolle diese annehmen, „wenn eine 2. Auflage des Werkes in Betracht kommen sollte" (Brief vom 18./30. März 1876). Tatsächlich wurde die ursprüngliche Fassung niemals in Partitur gedruckt, bis sie in Band 28 der Gesamtausgabe 1955 erschien. Jurgenson brachte eine vollständige Partitur erst im August 1879 heraus, die damals als 2. Auflage, „revidiert und korrigiert vom Komponisten" bezeichnet wurde. Eine wirkliche 2. Ausgabe der Fassung für zwei Klaviere erschien gleichzeitig in Übereinstimmung damit. Die Änderungen betreffen nur die Anlage der Klavierstimme im 1. Satz und geben vielleicht Dannreuthers Vorschläge wieder, deren Original verloren ist.

Von Dezember 1888 bis Februar 1889 bereitete Tschaikowsky in Beratung mit Siloti eine 3. Auflage des Konzerts vor. Hierbei nahm er, außer einigen kleinen Korrekturen im 1. und 3. Satz eine größere Änderung im Finale vor: die Einsetzung von fünf Takten (109–113 der jetzigen Ausgabe) für eine Partie von 17 Takten – die Tschaikowsky scherzend „die verfluchte Stelle" genannt hatte –, worin die springende Figur des Klaviers über dem Orchester erscheint. (Brief an Siloti, 27. Dezember 1888/8. Januar 1889). Derselbe Brief zeigt, dass bei einer Aufführung mit Sapellnikow in Hamburg, etwa ein Jahr vorher, er diese springende Figur zeitweilig ganz herausgenommen hatte. Die 3. Auflage des Konzerts erschien Ende 1889 oder Anfang 1890.

Viele der Änderungen, die Tschaikowsky machte, betreffen Tempo-Bezeichnungen. So war z. B. die ursprüngliche Bezeichnung der berühmten Introduktion *Andante non troppo*. Die Zeitangabe des folgenden *Allegro* wurde vom Komponisten von C in ¢ korrigiert. Aber seine Absicht ist nicht klar, denn seine zweisprachige Anweisung an den Dirigenten, wegen der Viertel-Triolen auf zwei zu schlagen, kommt erst viel später, wo die Anweisung *Alla breve* und die neue Zeitangabe erscheinen. Eine Anzahl der jetzigen Tempoänderungen sind Übersetzungen von Tschaikowskys Blaustiftzusätzen zum Autograph; z. B. *plus lent* bei Takt 186 des 1. Satzes, der jetzt als *Poco meno mosso* erscheint. Die Bezeichnung *Sostenuto molto* bei Takt 101 des Finales – das erste Auftreten der springenden Figur – erscheint weder im Manuskript noch in der ersten Ausgabe und ebenso wenig *Tempo I ma tranquillo* bei Takt 214. Aber eine unbekannte Hand hat *Tempo I* in das Manuskript eingezeichnet, und Tschaikowsky hat hinzugefügt: *mais peu plus lent*. Indessen wurden nicht alle Bleistiftnotizen Tschaikowskys im Druck berücksichtigt. Darunter ist die wiederholte Anweisung zu erwähnen, nicht zu eilen (*ne pressez pas le mouvement*) bei Takt 420 und 425 des 1. Satzes. In der ursprünglichen Ausgabe ist der mittlere Teil des 2. Satzes nicht *Prestissimo* bezeichnet, sondern *Allegro vivace assai*, und nach einem Brief von Tanejew an K. N. Igumnow von 1912 (gedruckt in *Sovjetskaja Musika*, 1946, Nr. 1, Seite 88/89) erklärt er dies für das richtige Tempo, *Prestissimo* sei zu schnell.

Aus Modests Biographie ist bekannt, dass dieser Teil auf einer französischen *Chansonette* basiert, „Il faut s'amuser, danser et rire", „die mein Bruder Anatol und ich zu Beginn der 70er Jahre beständig sangen", und dass das erste Allegro-Thema des Konzerts ein Teil einer Melodie ist, die von blinden, so genannten „Lyra-Sängern" in der Ukraine gesungen wurden:

Auch das erste Thema des Finales geht auf eine ukrainische Volksweise zurück, die Tschaikowsky in Rubets „Sbornik ukrainskich narodnich pesen" (St. Petersburg, 1872) gefunden hatte:

Gerald Abraham

Piano Concerto No. 1

Peter Ilyich Tchaikovsky
(1840–1893)
Op. 23

I. Allegro non troppo e molto maestoso

© 2007 Ernst Eulenburg Ltd, London
and Ernst Eulenburg & Co GmbH, Mainz

accelerando

poco riten.　　**a tempo**

Cadenza

Tempo I

10

rallent. Meno mosso

12

22

31

EAS 147

32

Poco accelerando

38

EAS 147

55

EAS 147

Tempo I

II. Andantino semplice

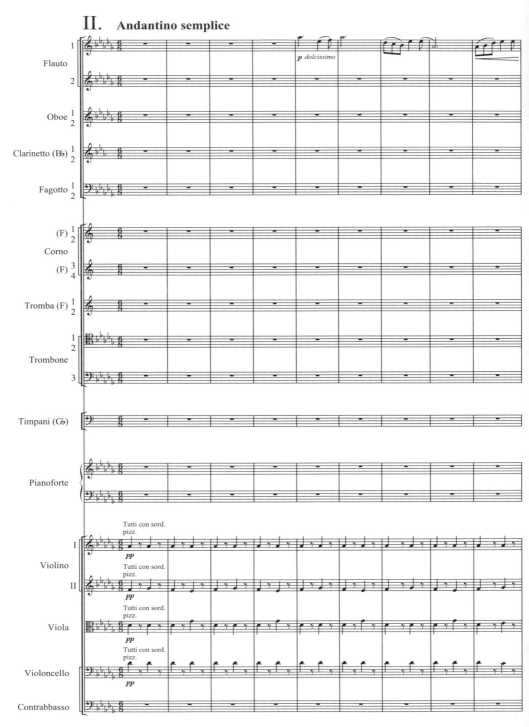

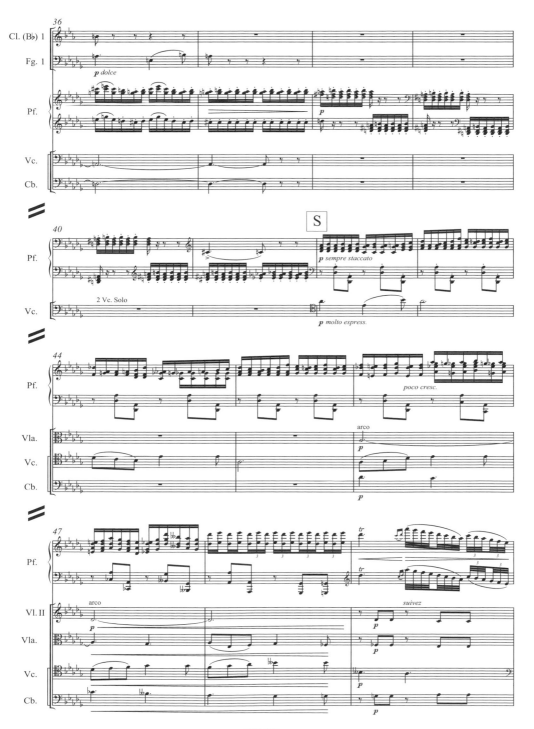

74

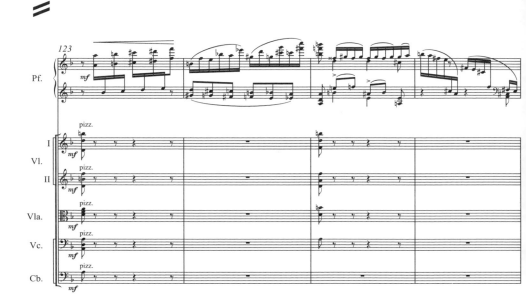

78

EAS 147

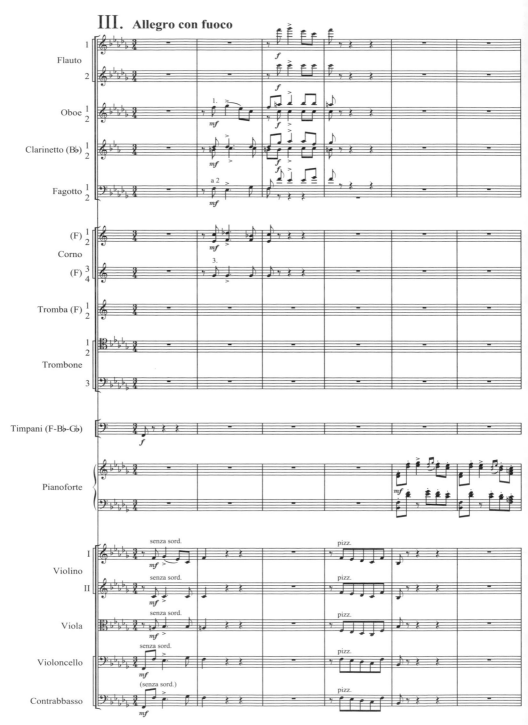

III. Allegro con fuoco

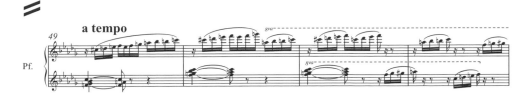

88

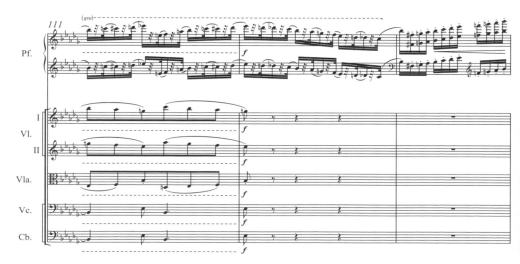

Tempo I, ma tranquillo

106

EAS 147

108

Molto meno mosso

EAS 147

Allegro vivo

114

EAS 147

Printed in China